"HA HA, HERMAN," CHARLIE BROWN

"HA HA, HERMAN," CHARLIE BROWN

A NEW PEANUTS BOOK

by Charles M. Schulz

HOLT, RINEHART AND WINSTON
New York • Chicago • San Francisco

Published simultaneously in Canada by Holt, Rinehart
and Winston of Canada, Limited.

First published in book form in 1972.

ISBN: 0-03-091405-1

Library of Congress Catalog Number: 79-183537

First Edition

Printed in the United States of America

Dear Pen Pal,
How have you been?

How are your mother and father? How are your brothers and sisters?

How are your Grandmothers and Grandfathers? How are your aunts and uncles? How are your Cousins? How are your second-cousins?

I NEVER KNOW WHERE TO STOP WITHOUT OFFENDING SOMEBODY

WHAT HAPPENS TO A LETTER AFTER YOU MAIL IT?

WELL, A MAN IN A SMALL TRUCK WILL PICK IT UP, AND TAKE IT TO THE POST OFFICE

FROM THERE IT WILL GO ON ANOTHER TRUCK TO ANOTHER OFFICE WHERE IT WILL GO TO THE AIRPORT WHERE IT WILL BE FLOWN TO NEW YORK

FROM NEW YORK IT WILL BE FLOWN OVER THE OCEAN WHERE ANOTHER TRUCK WILL...

WHAT ABOUT A SHUTE? I THOUGHT IT WENT DOWN A SHUTE..

WELL, YES, I GUESS IN NEW YORK IT GOES DOWN A SHUTE...

WHENEVER YOU TELL SOMETHING, YOU ALWAYS LEAVE SOMETHING OUT!

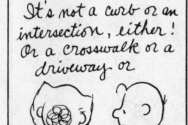

DO YOU THINK IT'S POSSIBLE FOR SOMEONE TO BE IN LOVE AND NOT KNOW IT?

YOU MEAN **ME**, DON'T YOU?

YOU'RE TALKING ABOUT ME, AREN'T YOU? WHY DON'T YOU COME RIGHT OUT AND SAY IT? WHY DON'T YOU ADMIT IT?

WHY DON'T YOU JUST ASK ME IF I THINK IT'S POSSIBLE THAT I'M IN LOVE WITH YOU, AND I DON'T KNOW IT?

SCHROEDER, DO YOU THINK IT'S POSSIBLE THAT YOU'RE IN LOVE WITH ME, AND YOU DON'T KNOW IT?

NO!

LOVE DRIVES ME CRAZY!

IF I TOLD YOU THAT WE WERE THROUGH WHEN I REALLY DIDN'T MEAN IT, WOULD WE STILL BE THROUGH?

IF I TOLD YOU THAT IT DIDN'T MATTER TO ME ONE WAY OR THE OTHER, WOULD WE STILL BE THROUGH?

WELL, IF I TOLD YOU THAT I MEANT I THOUGHT I KNEW THAT WE WERE THROUGH WHEN I SAID THAT YOU THOUGHT I KNEW I TOLD YOU WE WERE THROUGH, BUT I SAID WE...

LOVE IS NOT KNOWING WHAT YOU'RE TALKING ABOUT

Ecology Report

Ecology is everyone's business. We are all committed and we are all responsible.

P.S. This report was written on recycled paper.

THAT'S WHAT IS KNOWN AS TOUCHING ALL BASES!

THAT HAS TO BE THE WORST LANDING I'VE EVER SEEN..

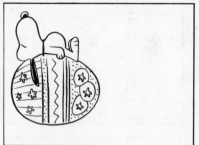

I'M STILL HUNGRY..

I ATE A PEANUT BUTTER SANDWICH, AN APPLE AND TWO COOKIES, BUT I'M STILL HUNGRY..

THAT ALWAYS USED TO BE ENOUGH FOR ME..

TRASH

I THINK I'VE OUTGROWN MY LUNCH!

HOW ABOUT A GAME OF MARBLES AFTER SCHOOL, FRANKLIN?

I CAN'T..I HAVE A GUITAR LESSON AT THREE-THIRTY...

RIGHT AFTER THAT I HAVE LITTLE LEAGUE, AND THEN SWIM CLUB, AND THEN DINNER AND THEN A '4 H' MEETING

I LEAD A VERY ACTIVE TUESDAY!

WHERE'S YOUR DOG?

HE WENT OFF SOME PLACE TO INTERVIEW MISS SWEETSTORY

HE'S GOING TO WRITE HER BIOGRAPHY

I READ A BIOGRAPHY OF ABRAHAM LINCOLN ONCE...

I DIDN'T LIKE IT, THOUGH, BECAUSE THE AUTHOR NEVER MENTIONED GEORGE WASHINGTON AND I'VE ALWAYS BEEN SORT OF INTERESTED IN GEORGE WASHINGTON

THAT MAKES MY HEAD HURT

YOUR DOG HAS NO RIGHT TO WALK OFF AND LEAVE YOU, CHARLIE BROWN!

YOU FEED HIM, AND YOU GIVE HIM A HOME...IN RETURN, IT'S HIS JOB TO GUARD YOUR PROPERTY, AND BE YOUR FRIEND! THE TROUBLE WITH YOU IS YOU DON'T KNOW HOW TO RAISE A DOG, CHARLIE BROWN!

HAVE YOU EVER RAISED A DOG?

OF COURSE NOT!! I WOULDN'T EVEN OWN A DOG!

ANOTHER UNMARRIED MARRIAGE COUNSELOR.. ❊ SIGH ❊

WHAT'S THAT? WHAT DID YOU SAY?

THERE IT IS! A VINE-COVERED COTTAGE WITH ROSE BUSHES, A WILLOW TREE AND A PICKET FENCE!

THERE IT STANDS, JUST AS I HAD IMAGINED IT! OH, MISS SWEETSTORY, I'VE FOUND YOU AT LAST!

WHEN SHE ANSWERS THE DOOR, I'LL REMOVE MY DOG DISH AS IF IT WERE A HAT, I'LL BOW AND IN A VERY DIGNIFIED MANNER I'LL SAY,...

"HI, SWEETIE!"

WHY DOES A PERSON OWN A DOG?

FOR SECURITY, I GUESS... FOR THE SECURITY OF KNOWING THAT THERE'S AT LEAST ONE CREATURE IN THE WORLD WHO LIKES YOU

WHAT IF THAT CREATURE WALKS OFF, AND LEAVES YOU?

YOU DON'T **LET** HIM LEAVE YOU, CHARLIE BROWN! YOU TIE HIM UP, OR LOCK HIM IN THE GARAGE!

YOU JUST DON'T UNDERSTAND SECURITY, CHARLIE BROWN

Panel 1
A Biography of
Helen Sweetstory

Panel 2
YOU'RE BACK! WHEN DID YOU GET BACK? DID YOU MEET MISS SWEETSTORY? DID YOU INTERVIEW HER? WHAT IS SHE LIKE?

Panel 3
DID SHE ANSWER ALL YOUR QUESTIONS? WAS SHE NICE?

Panel 4
DOES SHE REALLY LIVE IN A VINE-COVERED COTTAGE?

I MAY HAVE TO RENT A STUDIO DOWNTOWN..

Panel 5
Helen Sweetstory was born on a small farm on April 5, 1950.

Panel 6
I THINK I'LL SKIP ALL THE STUFF ABOUT HER PARENTS AND GRANDPARENTS...THAT'S ALWAYS KIND OF BORING...

Panel 7
I'LL ALSO SKIP ALL THE STUFF ABOUT HER STUPID CHILDHOOD... I'LL GO RIGHT TO WHERE THE ACTION BEGAN...

Panel 8
It was raining the night of her high-school prom.

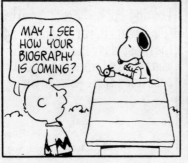

those years in Paris were to be among the finest of her life.

Looking back, she once remarked, "Those years in Paris were among the finest of my life." That was what she said when she looked back upon those years in Paris

where she spent some of the finest years of her life.

I THINK THIS IS GOING TO NEED A LITTLE EDITING...

THIS IS KIND OF AN INTERESTING ARTICLE

"MISS HELEN SWEETSTORY, AUTHOR OF THE 'BUNNY-WUNNY' SERIES, DENIED THAT THE STORY OF HER LIFE WAS BEING WRITTEN...'SUCH A BIOGRAPHY IS COMPLETELY UNAUTHORIZED' SHE SAID..."

WELL! WHAT DO YOU THINK OF THAT?

HERE'S THE WORLD WAR I FLYING ACE ZOOMING THROUGH THE AIR IN HIS SOPWITH CAMEL!

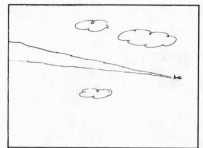

PSYCHIATRIC HELP 5¢

I WONDER IF IT'S POSSIBLE REALLY TO MAKE A FRESH START...

THE DOCTOR IS IN

PSYCHIATRIC HELP 5¢

THE DOCTOR IS IN

SEE THAT PLANE UP THERE?

IT'S FILLED WITH PEOPLE WHO ARE ALL GOING SOMEPLACE..THAT'S WHAT I'D LIKE TO DO.. GO OFF SOMEPLACE, AND START A NEW LIFE...

FORGET IT, CHARLIE BROWN...WHEN YOU GOT OFF THE PLANE, YOU'D STILL BE THE SAME PERSON YOU ARE...

HE DOCTOR

BUT MAYBE WHEN I GOT TO THIS NEW PLACE, THE NEW PEOPLE WOULD LIKE ME BETTER

ONLY UNTIL THEY GOT TO KNOW YOU, CHARLIE BROWN..THEN YOU'D BE RIGHT BACK WHERE YOU STARTED..

BUT MAYBE THESE NEW PEOPLE WOULD BE MORE UNDERSTANDING

PEOPLE ARE PEOPLE, CHARLIE BROWN...

THE DOCTOR IS IN

WELL, MAYBE I..

FORGET IT, CHARLIE BROWN

BUT..

THE DOCTOR IS IN

NOPE!

UH..

THE DOCTOR IS IN

FIVE CENTS, PLEASE

SIGH

THE DOCTOR IS IN

ONCE YOU HAVE A PATIENT HOOKED, LAND HIM!

THE DOCTOR IS IN

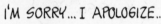

THERE I WAS..RESTING COMFORTABLY...

SUDDENLY I WAS PLAGUED BY A SELF-DOUBT!

HEY, SNOOPY, I NEED A FAVOR..

SOMETIMES, WHEN A PERSON ASKS ANOTHER PERSON TO DO A FAVOR, HE DOES IT SO THE OTHER PERSON CAN BE MADE TO FEEL GOOD BY DOING A FAVOR...

THEREFORE, IF THAT OTHER PERSON KNOWS HE IS BEING HELPED TO FEEL GOOD, HE SHOULD DO THE FAVOR FOR THAT PERSON SO HE ALSO WILL BE MADE TO FEEL GOOD

WHERE'D HE GO?

Z

IT'S ALL YOUR FAULT, CHARLIE BROWN, BECAUSE YOU OWN SUCH A STUPID BEAGLE!

DO YOU KNOW WHAT I JUST READ IN A MEDICAL JOURNAL?

IT SAID THAT A PERSON WHO IS DEPRIVED OF HIS BLANKET BY A STUPID BEAGLE WHO HAS IT MADE INTO A SPORT COAT CANNOT SURVIVE FOR MORE THAN FORTY-EIGHT HOURS!

THAT MUST BE AN INTERESTING MEDICAL JOURNAL..

PLEASE LET ME TOUCH MY BLANKET..

I KNOW IT'S YOUR SPORT COAT NOW... I DON'T DENY THAT, BUT I'VE GOT TO TOUCH IT...

YOU OWE ME THAT MUCH... I'M CRACKING UP, DON'T YOU SEE? I CAN'T LAST MUCH LONGER... LET ME TOUCH YOUR COAT..PLEASE!

KEEP AWAY...YOU'LL GET ME ALL WRINKLED!

AND THEN SHE'D KIND OF GRIN..

※ SIGH ※

I'M WORRIED ABOUT YOU, CHUCK

ABOUT ME?

YES, I'M WORRIED THAT YOU'RE LIVING TOO MUCH IN THE PAST...YOU HAVEN'T SEEN THAT LITTLE RED-HAIRED GIRL FOR OVER A YEAR, AND YET YOU KEEP TALKING ABOUT HER

MAYBE I'M LIVING IN THE FUTURE... MAYBE THAT'S WHAT WE CALL "HOPE"....OR MAYBE I'M JUST TOO WISHY-WASHY TO FORGET HER...

I DON'T KNOW, CHUCK... I JUST HATE TO SEE YOU ALWAYS LIVING IN THE PAST...OF COURSE, I'D HATE TO SEE YOU ONLY LIVING IN THE FUTURE, TOO...

MAYBE, AS THEY ALWAYS SAY, THE TRUTH LIES SOMEWHERE IN-BETWEEN..

THE TRUTH IS JUST AS WISHY-WASHY AS I AM!

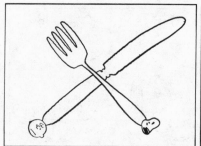

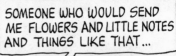

I HAVE A SUGGESTION TO MAKE.

I SUGGEST THAT THE BOARD OF EDUCATION BE TOLD TO BUY A HERD OF TWENTY-FOUR HORSES...

THEN, INSTEAD OF PLAYING A BUNCH OF STUPID GAMES DURING GYM CLASS, WE COULD ALL SADDLE UP, AND GO FOR LONG RIDES...

LOTS OF GOOD SUGGESTIONS NEVER GET OFF THE GROUND!

TAKE THAT, YOU STUPID SCHOOL!!

BOOT!

I LIKE SUMMER VACATION... IT'S THE ONLY TIME WHEN YOU CAN RUN RIGHT UP TO A SCHOOL AND KICK IT!

SHE DID IT! SHE HIT A HOME RUN!

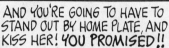
AND YOU'RE GOING TO HAVE TO STAND OUT BY HOME PLATE, AND KISS HER! YOU PROMISED!!

SHE'S ROUNDING FIRST...SHE'S ROUNDING SECOND..SHE'S ROUNDING THIRD..SHE'S HEADING FOR HOME! IT'S KISSING TIME! LA DE DA DE DA DE DA DE DA

LUCY HIT A HOME RUN!

OKAY, SCHROEDER, THIS IS IT! YOU PROMISED TO KISS HER..

A PROMISE IS A PROMISE...

FORGET IT! IF THAT'S THE ONLY WAY I'LL EVER GET YOU TO KISS ME, FORGET IT!

ANOTHER TRIUMPH FOR WOMEN'S LIB!

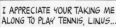

I APPRECIATE YOUR TAKING ME ALONG TO PLAY TENNIS, LINUS...

THAT'S THE ONLY TROUBLE WITH TENNIS.. YOU CAN'T PLAY IT ALONE

MAYBE WE WON'T GET TO PLAY AT ALL... THE COURTS ARE ALL FULL..

THE COURTS ARE ALWAYS FULL WITH BIG KIDS, AND THEY NEVER LET YOU PLAY... I HATE BIG KIDS! THEY NEVER GIVE YOU A CHANCE!

THEY'LL PLAY ALL DAY...JUST YOU WATCH! THEY'LL HOG THE COURTS ALL DAY! THEY'LL NEVER QUIT...THEY'LL JUST KEEP ON PLAYING AND PLAYING, AND THEY'LL NEVER...

YOU BIG KIDS GET OFF THAT COURT RIGHT NOW, OR MY BOY FRIEND WILL CLOBBER YOU!!

THAT'S THE ONLY TROUBLE WITH TENNIS... YOU CAN'T PLAY IT ALONE

HELLO, CHUCK? ARE YOU GOING TO CAMP THIS YEAR? I HEARD YOU WERE

ANYWAY, THE GIRLS' CAMP IS JUST ACROSS THE LAKE FROM THE BOYS' CAMP...

MAYBE I'LL SCAMPER AROUND THE OL' POND ON MY LITTLE PEGGY FLEMING LEGS AND VISIT YOU...OKAY? SEE YOU, CHUCK!

PEGGY FLEMING LEGS?

SO LONG, FRIEND..HAVE A GOOD TIME...

THERE GOES WOODSTOCK OFF TO EAGLE CAMP..

HE'S VERY AMBITIOUS..

HE HAS NO DESIRE TO END UP BEING A SPARROW..

AH, ANOTHER LETTER FROM WOODSTOCK WHO'S AT EAGLE CAMP

" DEAR FRIEND OF FRIENDS... TODAY WE HEARD A SPECIAL LECTURE BY A CATERPILLAR WHO HAD CRAWLED ALL THE WAY ACROSS A FREEWAY WITHOUT GETTING RUN OVER.. "

" IT WAS A VERY EXCITING ADVENTURE...HE HAD ALL OF US SITTING ON THE EDGE OF OUR BRANCHES! HA HA "

THAT WOODSTOCK!

HEY, PAL, THEY'RE HAVING A LITTLE ASTRONOMY CLASS TONIGHT..DO YOU WANNA GO?

SHUT UP AND LEAVE ME ALONE!

THAT KID IS BEGINNING TO GET TO ME...MAYBE HE NEEDS TO BE NEEDED...

HEY, PAL, I HATE TO GO TO THESE CAMP THINGS ALONE...COULD YOU HELP ME OUT, AND GO WITH ME?

SHUT UP, AND LEAVE ME ALONE!

I LOVE GOING TO SUMMER CAMP AND MAKING NEW FRIENDS...

IS LOVE A 'NOW' KIND OF THING, CHUCK, OR IS IT MOSTLY HOPE AND MEMORIES?

WELL, MY DAD SAYS THAT HE TOOK A GIRL TO THE MOVIES ONCE, AND IT WAS ONE OF THOSE REAL SAD LOVE STORIES...

HE REMEMBERED THAT ANNE BAXTER WAS IN IT, AND FOR YEARS AFTERWARD, EVERY TIME HE SAW ANNE BAXTER, HE'D GET REAL DEPRESSED BECAUSE IT WOULD REMIND HIM OF THAT MOVIE AND THE GIRL HE HAD BEEN WITH...

HE NEVER FORGOT THAT GIRL BECAUSE EVERY TIME HE SAW ANNE BAXTER, IT WOULD REMIND HIM OF HER...

THEN, ONE NIGHT ON THE LATE, LATE SHOW, THAT SAME MOVIE CAME ON, BUT IT TURNED OUT THAT HE HAD BEEN WRONG ALL THOSE YEARS... IT WASN'T ANNE BAXTER... IT WAS SUSAN HAYWARD!

LOVE HAS ITS MEMORIES, I GUESS

I WAS REALLY HOPING IT WAS A 'NOW' KIND OF THING

IT IS FOR SOME OF US, SWEETIE!

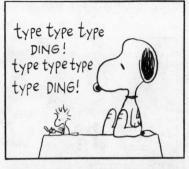

SIGH

OKAY, BALLOON, I'LL TELL YOU WHAT I'M GONNA DO..

?

I'M GOING TO LET YOU GO SO YOU CAN FLY AROUND FOR AWHILE AND GET A LITTLE EXERCISE, BUT YOU HAVE TO PROMISE TO COME BACK; OKAY?

THERE YOU GO!

HAHAHAHAHA

BOY, IF YOU'RE NOT THE STUPIDEST PERSON ALIVE, I DON'T KNOW WHO IS! "FLY AROUND FOR AWHILE AND GET A LITTLE EXERCISE, AND THEN COME BACK!" A BALLOON? WOW!

BALLOONS AND LITTLE BROTHERS DRIVE ME CRAZY!

SCHULZ

YOU SEEM BOTHERED BY SOMETHING, CHARLIE BROWN...

I KEEP HAVING THIS DAYDREAM.. I SEE MYSELF YEARS FROM NOW AT A HUGE BANQUET...

THE MASTER OF CEREMONIES IS INTRODUCING THE HEAD TABLE, AND WHEN HE GETS TO ME, I AM INTRODUCED AS A "FORMER GREAT"

BEFORE YOU CAN BE A "FORMER GREAT," CHARLIE BROWN, YOU HAVE TO BE A "GREAT"...

THAT'S WHAT BOTHERS ME!

PSYCHIATRIC HELP 5¢

THE DOCTOR IS [IN]

TROUBLE SEEMS TO FOLLOW ME EVERYWHERE

I CAN'T SEEM TO AVOID IT

THE DOCTOR IS [IN]

NO MATTER WHERE I AM, TROUBLE SEEMS TO FIND ME

WHAT YOU NEED, CHARLIE BROWN, IS AN UNLISTED LIFE!

THE DOCTOR IS [IN]

CAT FIGHT! DOG FIGHT!

CAT AND DOG FIGHT! IT'S A MASSACRE!!!

SNOOPY IS RESCUING WOODSTOCK! THE CAT NEXT DOOR GOT WOODSTOCK! SNOOPY IS RESCUING HIM!!

JUST WHAT I NEEDED...A FIGHT WITH A FIFTY-POUND CAT OVER AN OLD YELLOW GLOVE!

I APOLOGIZE, SNOOPY..

I THOUGHT THE CAT NEXT DOOR HAD GOTTEN WOODSTOCK, BUT IT WAS ONLY AN OLD YELLOW GLOVE...

BUT IT PROVED ONE THING, DIDN'T IT? IT PROVED YOU WERE WILLING TO GIVE YOUR LIFE FOR YOUR FRIEND! YOU COULD HAVE BEEN KILLED!

YOU THINK I'M ALIVE?

WELL, TODAY'S THE DAY I FACE THE STUDENT COUNCIL

THIS DRESS-CODE THING IS SO PIGGY!

FORTUNATELY, I'M NOT WORRIED ANY MORE BECAUSE I KNOW I HAVE A GOOD ATTORNEY...

MY PROBLEM IS I CAN NEVER TELL JOHN DOE FROM RICHARD ROE!

SCHULZ

MY NAME IS PATRICIA REICHARDT, AND I AM REPORTING TO THE STUDENT COUNCIL AS REQUESTED

I HAVE ALSO BROUGHT MY ATTORNEY WHO WILL BE ADVISING ME..

WHERE'S JOHN DOE AND RICHARD ROE? I THOUGHT THEY WERE GOING TO BE HERE..

YES, I'M PREPARED TO ANSWER ALL QUESTIONS

I THINK I SHOULD OPEN WITH AN IMPASSIONED PLEA AGAINST THE STAMP ACT

MY ATTORNEY WILL ADVISE ME OF MY RIGHTS...

"LET THE BUYER BEWARE!"

SCHULZ

THEY'RE DECIDING MY CASE NOW, SNOOPY...

WITHOUT YOUR HELP, I DOUBT IF I WOULD HAVE HAD A CHANCE

I REMEMBER MY MOST FAMOUS CASE.. JOHN DOE VERSUS RICHARD ROE! THAT RICHARD ROE WAS QUITE A GUY...

ACTUALLY, I'M VERY CONFIDENT... I HAVE FAITH IN THE JUDGMENT OF MY FELLOW HUMAN BEINGS, AND I'M SURE THAT WITH YOUR HANDLING OF MY CASE I'LL BE FOUND...

GUILTY!!

HELLO, CHUCK? LET ME TALK TO MY ATTORNEY, WILL YOU?

YEAH, I LOST THE CASE... I HAVE TO SPEND EACH LUNCH HOUR NOW STUDYING THE CONSTITUTION.. REAL PIGGY, HUH? OH, WELL, THE MORE I STUDY IT, THE MORE I'M CONVINCED I WAS RIGHT... ANYWAY, LET ME TALK TO MY ATTORNEY, WILL YOU?

YOUR CLIENT IS ON THE PHONE AGAIN..

I CAN'T TALK TO HER NOW... I'M DICTATING MY MEMOIRS!

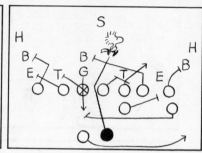

♪♪ CHARLIE BROWNNNN... ♪♪

I CAN'T BELIEVE IT!

CHARLIE BROWN, I'LL HOLD THE FOOTBALL, AND YOU COME RUNNING UP AND KICK IT...

I CAN'T BELIEVE IT! I CAN'T BELIEVE THAT ANYONE WOULD ACTUALLY THINK I'M THAT STUPID!

BUT YOU DON'T UNDERSTAND, CHARLIE BROWN...I REPRESENT AN ORGANIZATION, AND I'M HOLDING THIS BALL AS A REPRESENTATIVE OF THAT ORGANIZATION

IF SHE REPRESENTS AN ORGANIZATION, THEN I GUESS SHE MUST BE SINCERE...

AAUGH!

WHAM!

THIS YEAR'S FOOTBALL WAS PULLED AWAY FROM YOU THROUGH THE COURTESY OF WOMEN'S LIB!

SCHULZ

AND THEN I READ MY PAPER ON GULLY CATS TO THE WHOLE CLASS..

I TOLD ALL ABOUT HOW FIERCE GULLY CATS ARE, AND I EVEN THREW IN A BIT ABOUT HOW THEY ARE IMMUNE TO THE BITE OF THE DREADED QUEEN SNAKE

WHAT SORT OF A GRADE DID YOUR TEACHER GIVE YOU?

"NICE TRY"

WHAP!

I LOVE RAKING!

YES, MA'AM...
I'M READY...

THIS IS "SHOW AND
TELL" TIME...

FOR ALL YOU LUCKY KIDS OUT THERE IN
CLASSROOM-LAND I'VE BROUGHT MY
FAMOUS LEAF COLLECTION!

BUT FIRST, A WORD
FROM MY SPONSOR..

THESE LEAVES ARE
BROUGHT TO YOU
THROUGH THE COURTESY
OF OUR COUNTRY'S TREES

MY LEAF COLLECTION WAS GATHERED FROM
MANY LAWNS AND ALONG-SIDE MANY CURBS...
THESE ARE LEAVES FROM ALL WALKS OF LIFE...

AND NOW A BRIEF
WORD FROM MY
CO-SPONSOR,
THE RAIN...

THE RAIN COMES DOWN
FROM THE CLOUDS WHICH
ARE IN THE SKY, AND WATERS
THE SOIL UPON WHICH SIT
THE TREES WHEREON
GREW THESE LEAVES...

WHICH BRINGS US
BACK TO MY
FAMOUS COLLECTION..
YES, MA'AM?

FIRST THEY WANT YOU
TO SHOW AND TELL, AND
THEN THEY DON'T WANT
YOU TO SHOW AND TELL...

HI, CHUCK! GUESS WHO'S VISITING HERE WITH ME..

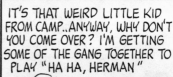

IT'S THAT WEIRD LITTLE KID FROM CAMP..ANYWAY, WHY DON'T YOU COME OVER? I'M GETTING SOME OF THE GANG TOGETHER TO PLAY "HA HA, HERMAN"

"HA HA, HERMAN"?

SIR, IS CHUCK THAT ROUND-HEADED KID I MET AT CAMP?

STOP CALLING ME "SIR"!

C'MON, SNOOPY.. WE'RE GOING TO PEPPERMINT PATTY'S HOUSE..

SHE'S INVITED US OVER FOR A GAME OF "HA HA, HERMAN"

REALLY?

THERE'S ONLY ONE THING THAT WILL GET ME TO WALK CLEAR ACROSS TOWN...

A ROUSING GAME OF "HA HA, HERMAN"!

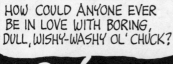

PSST, SIR! MAY I COME IN?

"PSST, SIR"? WHAT KIND OF AN EXPRESSION IS THAT? STOP CALLING ME "SIR"

I'VE JUST BEEN OVER TO SEE CHUCK.. HE'S PRETTY HURT... HE'S TAKEN TO HIS BED...

SO HAVE I...WHEN I THINK OF HOW I HURT HIS FEELINGS, I WANT TO DIE..I FEEL AWFUL... I REALLY OFFENDED HIM...

IN FIRST-AID CLASS I LEARNED THAT IF YOU HAVE OFFENDED SOMEONE, THE BEST TREATMENT IS TO APOLOGIZE IMMEDIATELY..

SCHULZ

I THINK THAT A HEARTFELT APOLOGY WILL WORK WONDERS

YOU SEE, CHUCK SIMPLY DOESN'T REALIZE THAT DEEP DOWN YOU'RE REALLY IN LOVE WITH HIM, AND..

I TOLD YOU I'M NOT IN LOVE WITH HIM! HOW COULD ANYONE LOVE SOMEONE AS WISHY-WASHY AS...

CAREFUL! NOW, YOU'RE RIGHT BACK WHERE YOU STARTED

INCIDENTALLY, HAVE YOU NOTICED THAT I STOPPED CALLING YOU "SIR"?

I CAN'T STAND IT!

SCHULZ

SO YOU SEE, CHUCK, I APOLOGIZE FOR SAYING THAT YOU'RE STUPID AND WISHY-WASHY AND EVERYTHING...

IT'S NOT EASY FOR A GIRL TO TALK LIKE THIS TO A BOY, YOU KNOW...

I KNOW, BUT I ALWAYS USED TO THINK HOW NICE IT WOULD BE IF THAT LITTLE RED-HAIRED GIRL WOULD JUST COME UP TO ME, AND..

I CAN'T STAND YOU, CHUCK!!!!

"HA HA HERMAN"

RICH MAN, POOR MAN..

BEGGAR MAN, THIEF...

..DOCTOR, LAWYER...

LAB TECHNICIAN, HAIR STYLIST, ACCOUNT EXECUTIVE, DENTAL ASSISTANT...

HERE WE ARE, SNOOPY, SITTING IN A PUMPKIN PATCH WAITING FOR THE "GREAT PUMPKIN"

EVERY HALLOWEEN THE GREAT PUMPKIN FLIES THROUGH THE AIR WITH HIS BAG OF TOYS

AND JUST THINK..IF YOU AND I SIT HERE ALL NIGHT, WE MAY GET TO SEE HIM!

I REALLY APPRECIATE YOUR SITTING OUT HERE WITH ME, SNOOPY...

I MUST ADMIT, HOWEVER, THAT I'VE BEEN WONDERING WHY YOU'RE WEARING THOSE DARK GLASSES...

THERE ARE CERTAIN TIMES WHEN YOU PREFER NOT TO BE RECOGNIZED!

I HOPE I HELPED HIM, BUT I DON'T KNOW...

TEN MINUTES BEFORE YOU GO TO A PARTY IS NO TIME TO BE LEARNING HOW TO DANCE!

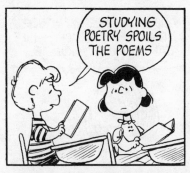

GENTLEMEN, ONCE AGAIN IT HAS COME TO MY ATTENTION THAT CERTAIN FOOD ITEMS ARE..

STOP SNOWING ON MY SECRETARY!!

A GOOD SECRETARY IS WORTH PROTECTING!

AAUGH!!

GOOD GRIEF! I CAN'T GET UP! I'M TRAPPED LIKE A TURTLE!

I CAN'T MOVE! I'M DOOMED... I'LL HAVE TO LIE HERE FOR THE REST OF MY LIFE!

AND THEN SHE TOLD ME ABOUT THIS ONE PARTY THEY HAD WHERE THEY PLAYED "SPIN THE BOTTLE"... EVERYONE SAT IN A CIRCLE WITH A MILK BOTTLE IN THE MIDDLE...

THEN THE PERSON WHO WAS "IT" WOULD SPIN THE BOTTLE LIKE THIS...

THEN THEY'D ALL SIT THERE AND WAIT FOR THE BOTTLE TO STOP SPINNING TO SEE WHO IT WOULD POINT TO..

IT SOUNDS LIKE A GREAT GAME... I WONDER WHO I'M POINTING TO...

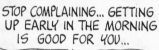

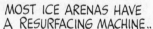

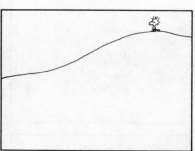

SOME FRIENDSHIPS ARE DOOMED FROM THE VERY BEGINNING!

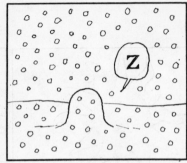

THAT'S WHAT HAPPENS WHEN YOU HAVE NO ANXIETIES...

SMAK!

OLD MOVIES SORT OF AFFECT ME THAT WAY..